D0907076

OCEAN
LIFE UP
CLOSE

Sea Stars

by Rebecca Pettiford

BLASTOFF!
READERS
3

BELLWETHER MEDIA • MINNEAPOLIS, MN

Note to Librarians, Teachers, and Parents:

Blastoff! Readers are carefully developed by literacy experts and combine standards-based content with developmentally appropriate text.

Level 1 provides the most support through repetition of high-frequency words, light text, predictable sentence patterns, and strong visual support.

Level 2 offers early readers a bit more challenge through varied simple sentences, increased text load, and less repetition of high-frequency words.

Level 3 advances early-fluent readers toward fluency through increased text and concept load, less reliance on visuals, longer sentences, and more literary language.

Level 4 builds reading stamina by providing more text per page, increased use of punctuation, greater variation in sentence patterns, and increasingly challenging vocabulary.

Level 5 encourages children to move from "learning to read" to "reading to learn" by providing even more text, varied writing styles, and less familiar topics.

Whichever book is right for your reader, Blastoff! Readers are the perfect books to build confidence and encourage a love of reading that will last a lifetime!

This edition first published in 2017 by Bellwether Media, Inc.

No part of this publication may be reproduced in whole or in part without written permission of the publisher. For information regarding permission, write to Bellwether Media, Inc., Attention: Permissions Department, 5357 Penn Avenue South, Minneapolis, MN 55419.

Library of Congress Cataloging-in-Publication Data

Names: Pettiford, Rebecca.
Title: Sea Stars / by Rebecca Pettiford.
Description: Minneapolis, MN : Bellwether Media, Inc., 2017. | Series:
  Blastoff! Readers. Ocean Life Up Close | Audience: Ages 5-8. | Audience:
  K to grade 3. | Includes bibliographical references and index.
Identifiers: LCCN 2015047015 | ISBN 9781626174214 (hardcover : alk. paper)
Subjects: LCSH: Starfishes–Juvenile literature.
Classification: LCC QL384.A8 P48 2017 | DDC 593.9/3–dc23
LC record available at http://lccn.loc.gov/2015047015

Printed in the United States of America, North Mankato, MN.

Table of Contents

What Are Sea Stars?

noduled
sea stars

Sea stars are **echinoderms** with **spiny** skin. They are often called starfish, but they are not fish.

There are about 2,000 different types of sea stars. They are found on the ocean floor and in **coral reefs**.

sunflower
star

paddle-spined
sea star

Sea stars come in many colors.
They are purple, red, pink, orange,
or white. Some are blue!

They range in size from about 0.4 inches (1 centimeter) to 3 feet (1 meter) from arm to arm.

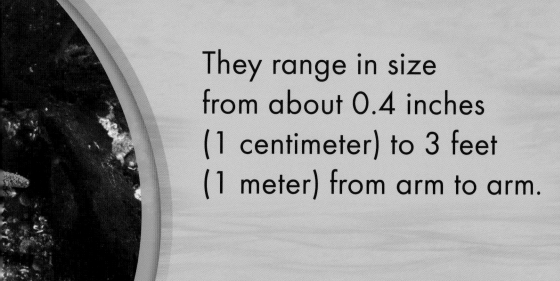

Sea Star Sizes

Smallest	Largest
paddle-spined sea star	sunflower star

actual size

average human

up to 0.4 inches (1 centimeter) from arm to arm	3 feet (1 meter) from arm to arm

Rays and Tube Feet

Five or more arms, called **rays**, are attached to a sea star's **central disk**. If a sea star loses a ray, a new one grows.

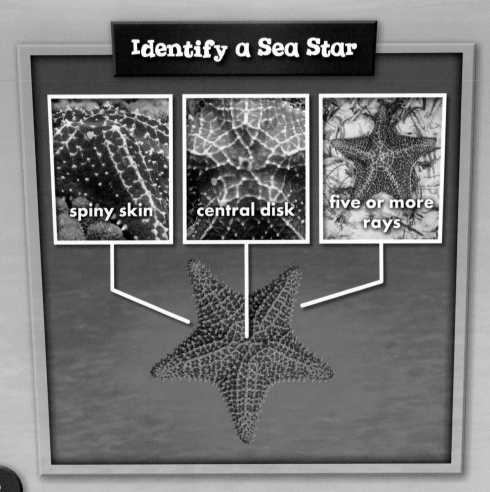

Identify a Sea Star

spiny skin

central disk

five or more rays

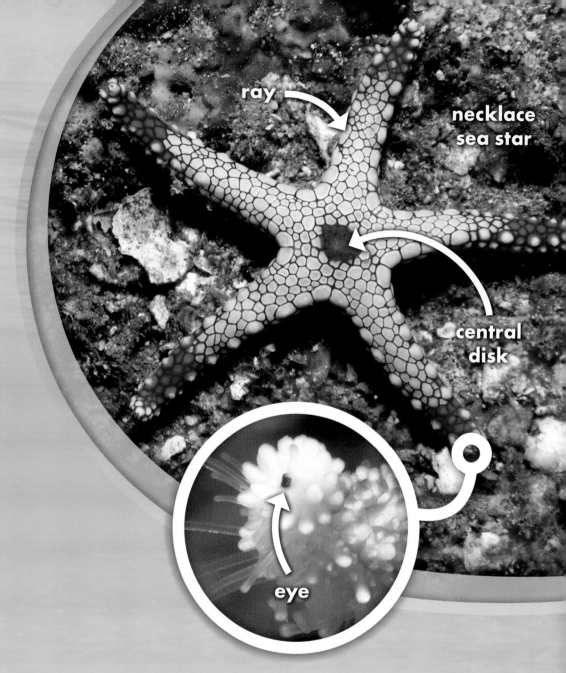

ray

necklace
sea star

central
disk

eye

Each ray has an eye on its tip.
Sea stars use their eyes to stay
close to the reef.

Sea stars have tube feet on the underside of their rays. The tube feet pump water to make the sea stars move.

sucker

tube feet

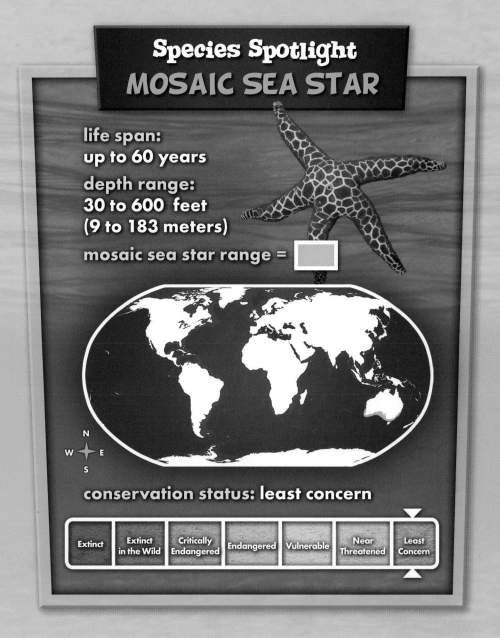

life span:
up to 60 years

depth range:
**30 to 600 feet
(9 to 183 meters)**

mosaic sea star range =

N
W E
S

conservation status: **least concern**

| Extinct | Extinct in the Wild | Critically Endangered | Endangered | Vulnerable | Near Threatened | Least Concern |

Suckers are at the end of each foot. These help sea stars attach to rocks and reefs.

Stomaching Clams

Sea stars are **carnivores**. They feed on slow-moving animals.

They use their strong sense of smell to find **prey**. Clams are a favorite food.

Catch of the Day

soft-shell clams

Mediterranean mussels

Pacific oysters

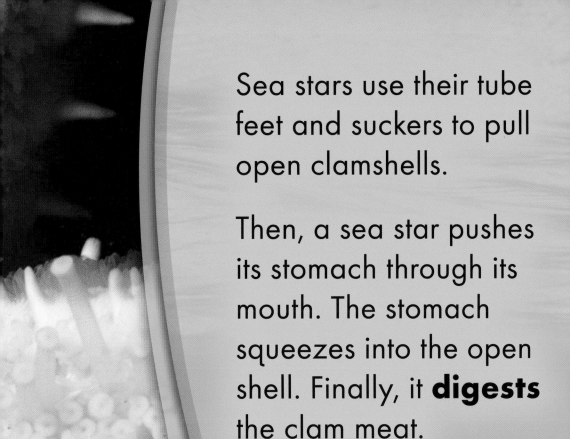

Sea stars use their tube feet and suckers to pull open clamshells.

Then, a sea star pushes its stomach through its mouth. The stomach squeezes into the open shell. Finally, it **digests** the clam meat.

stomach

Life of a Star

Sea stars hide to escape **predators**. They may bury themselves in sand.

Their spiny, colorful skin helps them blend in with coral reefs.

red comb
sea star

Sea Enemies

sea otters

herring gulls

Port Jackson sharks

warty sea star

Female sea stars can lay millions of eggs at a time. Tiny babies grow from the eggs.

These **larvae** float to find food. They start to look like sea stars after about three weeks.

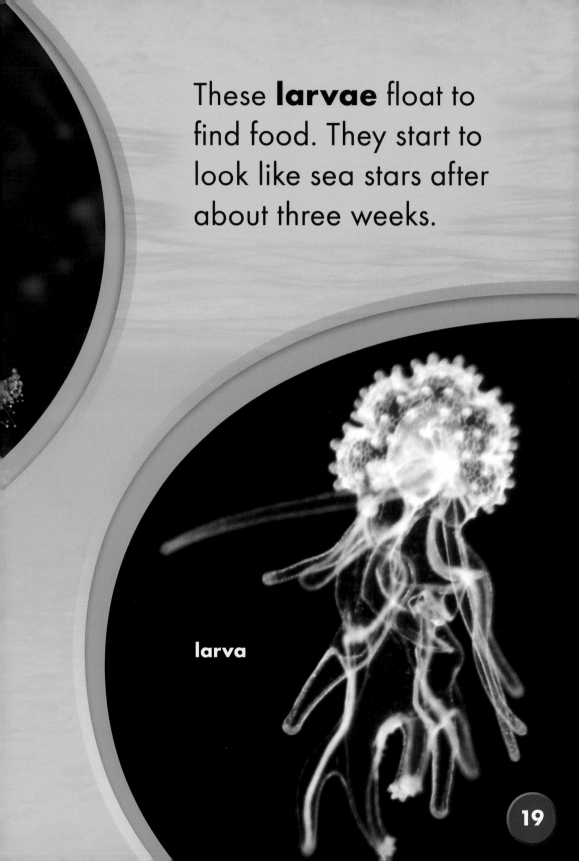

larva

Some sea stars make new life by splitting in two. When this happens, a new sea star forms.

Soon, there are two sea stars
instead of one!

Glossary

carnivores—animals that only eat meat

central disk—the middle circle of a sea star's body

coral reefs—structures made of coral that usually grow in shallow seawater

digests—breaks down food so it can be used for the body

echinoderms—ocean animals that pump water instead of blood; sea stars and sea urchins are echinoderms.

larvae—early, tiny forms of an animal that must go through a big change to become adults

predators—animals that hunt other animals for food

prey—animals that are hunted by other animals for food

rays—arms on sea stars

spiny—sharp and pointed

suckers—body parts that suck or cling

To Learn More

AT THE LIBRARY

Gibbs, Maddie. *Sea Stars.* New York, N.Y.:
PowerKids Press, 2014.

James, Helen Foster. *Discover Sea Stars.* Ann Arbor,
Mich.: Cherry Lake Publishing, 2016.

Schuh, Mari. *Sea Stars.* North Mankato, Minn.:
Capstone Press, 2016.

ON THE WEB

Learning more about sea stars
is as easy as 1, 2, 3.

1. Go to www.factsurfer.com.

2. Enter "sea stars" into the search box.

3. Click the "Surf" button and you will see a
   list of related web sites.

With factsurfer.com, finding more
information is just a click away.

Index

The images in this book are reproduced through the courtesy of: Kletr, front cover, p. 3; aquapix, pp. 4-5, 9 (top); Vilainecrevette, pp. 5 (top), 8 (top left, top right); e2dan, p. 5 (center); Deborah Coles, p. 5 (bottom); Greg Amptman, p. 6 (top); Mark O'Loughlin/ Wikipedia, p. 6 (bottom); Ethan Daniels, p. 8 (top center); MissRuby, p. 8 (bottom); Sanamyan/ Alamy, p. 9 (bottom); Deposit Photos/ Glow Images, p. 10 (top, bottom); Irko Van Der Heide, p. 11; Joe Belanger, p. 12; Mark Conlin/ SuperStock, p. 13; Yuriy Kvach/ Wikipedia, p. 14 (top left); DNetromphotos, p. 14 (top center); William C Bunce, p. 14 (top right); Age Fotostock/ SuperStock, p. 14 (bottom); Georgia Walters, p. 15; NHPA / Photoshot/ SuperStock, p. 16; David Litman, p. 17 (top left); Wolfgang Kruck, p. 17 (top center); Olivier Cochard-Labbé/ Wikipedia, p. 17 (top right); Ethan Daniels, p. 17 (bottom); Fred Bavendam/ Minden Pictures/ SuperStock/ Corbis, pp. 18, 20; FLPA/ SuperStock, p. 19; Hans Leijnse/ NiS/ Minden Pictures/ Corbis, p. 21.